MOR CONQUEROR

ENDORSEMENTS

This wonderful, little book will bless many parents and children as they face the huge challenges of anxiety. It's biblical and practical and gives children exercises that work. In fact, some adults will find the solutions are just what they need to deal with their own challenges!

DR. SCOTT TURANSKY
co-founder of the National Center for Biblical Parenting and co-author of fifteen books, including *Parenting is Heart Work*

This book is an essential resource for parents of children battling worry and anxiety. Laura Kuehn offers practical, action-oriented guidance to help parents and children work together to win the war against worry. I am recommending it every chance I get.

BENJAMIN RATTRAY, D.O., MBA, CPE, FAAP
Author of *When All Becomes New: A Doctor's Stories of Life, Love, and Loss*

MORE THAN A CONQUEROR

A Christian Kid's Guide to Winning the War Against Worry

LAURA KUEHN, LCSW

AMBASSADOR INTERNATIONAL
GREENVILLE, SOUTH CAROLINA & BELFAST, NORTHERN IRELAND

www.ambassador-international.com

MORE THAN A CONQUEROR
A Christian Kid's Guide to Winning the War Against Worry
©2023 by Laura Kuehn, LCSW
All rights reserved

Hardcover ISBN: 978-1-64960-487-3
Paperback ISBN: 978-1-64960-309-8
eISBN: 978-1-64960-331-9

No part of this publication may be reproduced, distributed, or transmitted in any form or by any means, including photocopying, recording, or other electronic or mechanical methods, without the prior written permission of the publisher, except in the case of brief quotations embodied in critical reviews and certain other noncommercial uses permitted by copyright law. For permission requests, contact the publisher using the information below.

Disclaimer: The contents of this book are not a substitute to professional assessment or treatment of mental or emotional disorders. Rather it is a forestep aiding the individual in self-identification of the effects of personal choice in contributing to their present life situation. It assumes that each individual is capable of making life enhancing decisions and encourages the reader to seek help of their doctor and a professional psychiatrist.

Cover design by Christopher Jackson
Interior typesetting by Dentelle Design
Edited by Katie Cruice Smith
Illustrations by Tincho Schmidt

Scripture quotations taken from THE HOLY BIBLE, NEW INTERNATIONAL VERSION®, NIV® Copyright © 1973, 1978, 1984, 2011 by Biblica, Inc.® Used by permission. All rights reserved worldwide.

AMBASSADOR INTERNATIONAL	AMBASSADOR BOOKS
Emerald House	The Mount
411 University Ridge, Suite B14	2 Woodstock Link
Greenville, SC 29601	Belfast, BT6 8DD
United States	Northern Ireland, United Kingdom
www.ambassador-international.com	www.ambassadormedia.co.uk

The colophon is a trademark of Ambassador, a Christian publishing company.

DEDICATION

For the child reading this book:

you have been on my mind and in my prayers from the beginning.

CONTENTS

INTRODUCTION 11

AUTHOR'S NOTE TO PARENTS AND
CAREGIVERS 13

AUTHOR'S NOTE TO KIDS. 17

SECTION 1: WHAT YOU NEED TO KNOW ABOUT WORRY . 19

WHAT IS WORRY? 21

YOUR BRAIN AND WORRY. 25

WHEN WORRY TAKES OVER 27

GOD'S DESIGN 31

SECTION 2: WORRY AND YOU. 33

THINGS THAT MAKE YOU FEEL WORRIED . . 35

YOUR WORRY BODY SIGNALS 37

HOW WORRY AFFECTS YOU AND YOUR
FAMILY. 39

KNOW YOUR ENEMY. 41

SECTION 3: TIME FOR WAR! 45

BATTLE #1: READY, SET, BREATHE! 47

BATTLE #2: DON'T JUST STAND THERE—GET
MOVING!. 51

BATTLE #3: CREATE PEACE—USE YOUR
IMAGINATION!. 55

BATTLE #4: ROUNDING UP THE ENEMY—
CREATE A WORRY BOX. 61

BATTLE #5: AVOID SURPRISE ATTACKS—
SCHEDULE YOUR WORRY TIME 65

BATTLE #6: TRAIN FOR BATTLE—FOOD,
WATER, SLEEP, AND EXERCISE 69

BATTLE #7: START OFF YOUR DAY RIGHT—PUT
ON THE ARMOR OF GOD 75

BATTLE #8: DON'T GET BRAINWASHED—TAKE
EVERY THOUGHT CAPTIVE! 83

BATTLE #9: FACE THE TRUTH WITH THANKS . 87

BATTLE #10: STAND YOUR GROUND—LOOK
YOUR WORRIES IN THE EYE 91

THE FINAL VERDICT: REMEMBER—THE WAR'S ALREADY WON......95

SECTION 4: THE ENEMY SURRENDERS! YOU'VE WON!...97

   KEEP YOUR GUARD(S) UP...........101

   CERTIFICATE OF VICTORY...........105

   ADDITIONAL DAILY LOGS...........107

   RECOMMENDED RESOURCES.........111

   ACKNOWLEDGMENTS..............113

   ABOUT THE AUTHOR...............115

*Who shall separate us from the love of Christ? Shall trouble or hardship or persecution or famine or nakedness or danger or sword? ... No, in all these things **we are more than conquerors through him who loved us**. For I am convinced that neither death nor life, neither angels nor demons, neither the present nor the future, nor any powers, neither height nor depth, nor anything else in all creation, will be able to separate us from the love of God that is in Christ Jesus our Lord.*

— Romans 8:35, 37-39 (emphasis mine)

INTRODUCTION

AUTHOR'S NOTE TO PARENTS AND CAREGIVERS

It can be very unsettling to be a parent or caregiver of an anxious child. At this point, you have likely prayed over him, held him close, and done everything else you can think of to help ease his worries. But despite your efforts, the worries remain. Maybe you have started to wonder if your child needs counseling. Or maybe you have sought counseling but have been put on a waiting list. Either way, you have chosen the right book. *More Than a Conqueror* was written to provide you with the insights, structure, and tools necessary to help guide your child through his or her battle with anxiety. It is grounded in Scripture and a hope in a God Who heals.

This workbook is intended to be completed collaboratively with your child over a period of about four weeks. As you know, all children are different, so you should feel free to go at a pace that is comfortable for your child.

You may be tempted to give this workbook to your child to do on his own. Depending upon your child's age or temperament, he may even ask to do it alone. However, it is best to present this workbook as a joint effort. Entering into this struggle with your child will create a strong alliance in his war against worry. Furthermore, if you struggle with issues related to worry, you can model success for your child by implementing some of the strategies in this book yourself.

WHAT IF HE GETS WORSE?

If you find that your child is not responding positively to the tasks in this book or if your child's anxiety level becomes too difficult for you to manage, please talk to your pediatrician right away or contact a crisis hotline. In most states, all you have to do is call 211. Your child could then complete this workbook in counseling sessions where his worries can be safely explored and contained.

WHAT IF HE DOESN'T WANT TO DO IT?

If your child resists starting this workbook, explore the reasons for his resistance. Does he experience any hidden "benefits" from worrying? What will he lose if his worries go away? What does he like about keeping the worries close? Sometimes, people want to hang on to what is familiar, even if it isn't good for them.

You might try gently pointing out how his worries are limiting him. Does he avoid certain events? Does he have physical symptoms that impact his day (stomachaches, difficulty sleeping, etc.)? Tell him you are in it with him and will battle his worries together.

Leave the workbook in an area where he can flip through and explore it on his own. You want to gently and consistently encourage him to participate. In the midst of a particular worry, you could say something like, "I bet that worry workbook has some tools that would be helpful for times like this." He will soon discover that the war on worry is a winnable one—with you and the Lord on his side.

AUTHOR'S NOTE TO KIDS

You may be wondering if this workbook is right for you. You may wonder if your problem with worry is really "that bad." Before you decide, ask yourself the following questions:
- Do I have fears about lots of different things?
- Do I spend a lot of time thinking about "what if" situations?
- Do I get stomachaches or headaches or have a hard time relaxing?
- Do I have a hard time concentrating because I'm thinking of what is coming next?
- Do I avoid taking risks or trying new things?
- Do I worry about making mistakes or getting criticized by others?
- Do I spend a lot of time thinking about things I can't control (wars, disasters, etc.)?
- Do I wonder if bad things that happen to others are going to happen to me?
- Do I worry a lot about my grades at school?

If you answered yes to only one or two of these worries and they don't happen very often, this book may not be for you. But if you find yourself dealing with a lot of the worries on this list most days and if they are taking up a lot of your energy, this book is going to be a big help.

You are not alone. A lot of kids struggle with the same kinds of worries as you. In this book, we are going to talk a lot about fighting the Worry Weasels. These guys love to make your worries and fears grow bigger and bigger. They want to keep you scared and trapped by your worries, unable to experience all that life has to offer. God has so much more in store for you, and He is powerful enough to help you!

This workbook contains a number of activities for you to complete with your parent or caregiver. I will refer to this helper as your "parent" throughout this book, but any caring adult you trust can work through this book with you. By the end, you will have collected a great big stockpile of weapons to help you fight and win your war against worry.

So, take a deep breath. Things are going to begin to get better very soon. That is because you are *"more* than a conqueror" through God, Who loves you!

SECTION 1

WHAT YOU NEED TO KNOW ABOUT WORRY

You may be tempted to skip these next two sections and head right for section three, which has all the weapons that you will need to fight off the Worry Weasels. It's understandable that you want relief, but it is important that you complete sections one and two first. It will really help you to better understand what is happening inside you when you worry. Understanding is the first step toward victory.

WHAT IS WORRY?

Worry (also called anxiety or nervousness) is actually a normal response to stress that everyone has. Yes, *everyone*. In small amounts, it can be rather helpful. Think about it this way: if you never worried in response to stress, you wouldn't feel the need to run away—even if a bear was chasing you! You would just think, *Oh, what a cute brown bear.* And the next thing you'd know, you'd be lunch.

Things that all humans do without thinking or deciding are called INSTINCTS. If you touch a hot pan, you will immediately pull your hand away. That is one type of instinct. The type of instinct that kicks into gear when you face something stressful or scary (like an angry bear) is called the FIGHT-OR-FLIGHT RESPONSE. This means that, without thinking, you will either stay and fight or turn and run.

Here are some other examples of this type of instinct at work:
- A mother runs in front of a speeding car to save her child (fight).
- A boy runs from a growling dog (flight).
- A dad goes into a house that is on fire to rescue his son (fight).
- You jump back when you get startled (flight).

Can you think of any more examples of fight-or-flight instincts? Write or draw them here:

Whether you stay and fight or turn and run, some physical changes start to happen in your body right away. Here are a few:
- Your heart may beat faster (to get blood to your muscles quickly).
- You may start breathing faster (so your muscles can get more oxygen).
- Your mouth may become dry (because moisture is needed elsewhere).
- Your hands may get cold (because blood flows to more important parts of your body).

- You may feel hot (because your body is working hard).
- You may start to sweat (your body's way of cooling down).
- You may feel lightheaded or have wobbly legs (due to too much oxygen from breathing too fast).
- You may feel like you have to go to the bathroom (because pressure builds up inside the body).

Have you experienced any of these when your flight-or-flight instinct kicks in? We will talk more about what it feels like for you in the next section, but first, you need to learn a little more about what is happening inside your brain.

YOUR BRAIN AND WORRY

Now, your brain is a very fancy organ. In fact, God has made it so fancy and so complicated that even doctors and scientists don't know *exactly* how it works. They do know, however, that different parts of the brain have different jobs.

One part of your brain has the job of kicking off those fight-or-flight instinctive reactions about which you just learned. Its job is to keep you safe in the face of danger. Another part is in charge of DECISION-MAKING. Its job is to help you think things through and weigh the good and bad of any situation. Here are some examples of the decision-making part of your brain at work:

- *I really like pizza, but I think I have had enough. I'll have some salad instead.*
- *I really want to watch this TV show, but I know it is scary and may give me nightmares. I'll watch a comedy instead.*
- *A lot of my classmates are starting to say bad words. I know that kind of talk isn't pleasing to God, so I will ask God to help me watch what I say.*

- *That thunder outside is very loud, but I know that I am safe in my house with my family.*

The fight-or-flight response was designed to work together with the decision-making part. If you have ever watched a swim competition or a running race, you might be familiar with false starts. This happens when an athlete takes off before the official has hit the buzzer or sounded the gun. When the athlete realizes his error, he walks (or swims) back to the starting line. The same sort of thing happens between these two parts of your brain.

Let's say you are sitting at the kitchen table, and a book slides off the counter behind you and lands with a thud. What do you do? You jump. That's the fight-or-flight part of your brain kicking into gear to keep you safe in the face of danger. But almost immediately (when you swing your head around to look), the decision-making part of your brain makes sense of all you see. There was a huge pile of papers that started to tip, and the heavy book on top slipped off and onto the floor. Instantly, you relax. There is no danger. You carry on with your lunch without giving it a second thought. You had experienced a false start to the fight-or-flight response, but the decision-making part told it to go back to the starting line.

This is how it is supposed to work, but sometimes, worry takes over. We will explore that next.

WHEN WORRY TAKES OVER

Whenever you are at war, it's important to know who your enemy is. In this war against worry, we are going to call our enemies the WORRY WEASELS. Their biggest goal is to turn those false starts into a full fight-or-flight reaction.

For some people who have seen or experienced a lot of scary things in their lives, the fight-or-flight response is very easy to turn on. So even though a book falling on the floor is not dangerous, the sound of it might instantly bring back memories of something that was. The Worry Weasels see this as their opportunity to get to work and will use those memories to fuel that false start. They want you to think you are in danger, even when you are not.

For other people, just a simple thought or feeling is powerful enough to create a false start. Nothing scary has to happen. They don't need to be startled. They can just have an anxious feeling or think an anxious thought. And unless the brain's decision-making part shuts it down, a full fight-or-flight response can kick into gear. Here's a diagram of what can happen:

THE WORRY CYCLE

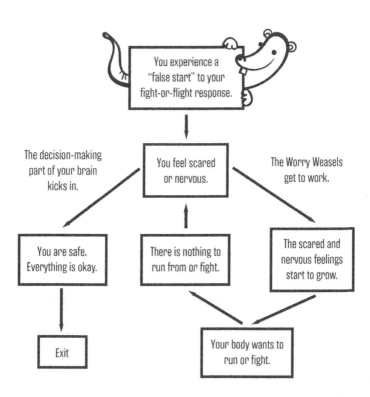

As you can see, the Worry Weasels want those anxious thoughts and feelings to get stuck in the worry cycle with nowhere to go. They just keep going round and round, getting bigger and bigger because you can't run away from your thoughts or feelings. Your instincts keep saying, *Danger! Danger! You'd better run! You'd better fight!* But there is nowhere to go. There is no one to fight.

Throughout this book, we are going to learn the different ways to combat the Worry Weasels. You will learn how to keep that cycle from starting or how to stop it if it does. But first, let's take a look at how God sees you.

GOD'S DESIGN

After learning all of this, you might be wondering why the decision-making part of your brain isn't doing a better job. It is important for you to know that God designed you the way He did for a reason. He knows you inside and out—just like you know every piece of that LEGO® set you put together. And He didn't make a single mistake when He made you. In fact, most people who struggle with worry are very sensitive and caring people. In that way, you are made in God's image.

Grab your Bible and take some time to read Psalm 139 with your parent right now. When you are done, list some things that God knows about you based on the passage.

1)

2)

3)

4)

Did you see verse fourteen? It says that you are a work of God and that all of His works are wonderful! After He made you, He sat back and smiled. You are His creation, and because of that, He is able to help you fight the war against worry. This book is going to give you the tools to do just that.

An important part of this war is figuring out exactly which specific worries bother you and how they make you feel inside your body. We are going to work on that next.

SECTION 2
WORRY AND YOU

In this section, you are going to do a lot of noticing exercises. Take your time with this section. The information you get from it will be very helpful later on. It is important to be honest with yourself and your parent about the different worries you have. And it is also important that you feel listened to by your parent and that you feel comfortable sharing these very personal things. (Note to parents: if you have never done so, now would be a good time to do some reading about empathic listening. There are a few resources listed at the end of the book for your reference.)

THINGS THAT MAKE YOU FEEL WORRIED

The first step is to name all the different worries you battle. Draw yourself in the box on the opposite page. On the lines following, write down the things about which you worry. There are no "wrong" or "bad" worries. Just list the different situations or thoughts that make you feel anxious. If you run out of lines, just add more. This is the time to be really honest.

After you make your list, put a number next to each worry. Put a "1" next to the worry that bothers you the most, a "2" next to the one that comes next, and so on. Take your time with this exercise, and feel free to come back and add to it or edit it if needed.

_____

_____

_____

_____

_____

_____

YOUR WORRY BODY SIGNALS

Next, it's time to start paying attention to how the Worry Weasels make you feel. The best way you can do this is to notice what is happening in your body when you get nervous. Then you will know how to fight back.

If you've never paid attention to what happens in your body when you are worried, this may take some time. Be patient and take a day to just listen to your body. Your parent may ask you, "Where in your body are you feeling the worries?" or "What is happening in your body right now?" when you seem nervous or anxious. Circle any worry signals you notice below.

Draw a picture of yourself again in the box on the following page. Then, once you have had time to observe your body signals, grab a pencil and draw a line from your circled worry signals to where you feel them in your body. Use a highlighter to mark the ones that happen most often. Feel free to add your own body signals, too.

SHARP PAIN IN THE CHEST
DIZZINESS OR LIGHTHEADEDNESS
LUMP IN THROAT (DIFFICULTY SWALLOWING)
SWEATY HANDS OR FEET
WOBBLY LEGS
RAPID BREATHING
FAST OR HARD HEARTBEAT
ALL-OVER SHAKINESS
STOMACHACHE
DRY MOUTH
BUTTERFLIES IN STOMACH
HAVE TO GO TO THE BATHROOM
DIFFICULTY CATCHING BREATH
NAUSEATED

HOW WORRY AFFECTS YOU AND YOUR FAMILY

If you struggle to fight off the Worry Weasels, chances are your family struggles right along with you. Because these feelings are so strong, your behavior is probably affected. Remember the fight-or-flight response? Remember how we said that you can't fight or run from your worries? That is true. But when your body is all geared up to do one of those things, you might start fighting or fleeing in other ways. Here are some common ways that kids just like you try to deal with the Worry Weasels:

The FLIGHT ways kids deal with Worry Weasels:
- Go to their room
- Stay away from people or large crowds
- Refuse to do things that they are told to do
- Stop talking
- Give up doing the things they enjoy most

The FIGHT ways kids deal with Worry Weasels:
- Break things
- Feel irritable or moody

- Snap at others
- Yell at others or start fights
- Hit or hurt others

How do you act when you feel overwhelmed with worry? Write your answers below. Cover your answers and then ask your parent to make a list of what behaviors *they* notice when you are worried. Compare your lists and talk about them together. Did your parent notice things you didn't? Now talk with your parent about if the way you are dealing with your worries is helping or hurting you.

MY LIST:

MY PARENT'S LIST:

KNOW YOUR ENEMY

When soldiers are getting ready to fight in a war, they study their enemy. They learn where their enemy lives, what they look like, and what weapons they use to fight. If you are going to win this war against worry (and you are!), then you need to know what those Worry Weasels look like and what they sound like. Take a few minutes to use your imagination and think about what your Worry Weasels look like. Draw them below. (Don't skip this, even if you think it is silly. It will help.)

When you can picture something, it takes the mystery out of it. It's like when you hear a weird noise in your house.

When you don't know what is causing it or where it is coming from, it can be a bit scary. Once you realize it's just the cat pawing at his food dish, your fear goes away.

From now on, when you think of the Worry Weasels, picture the drawing you made. Some kids like to make photocopies of the Worry Weasels, write a worry on the back of each one, and then tear them up into little pieces. Or they put the picture on the ground and stomp on it. (But don't stomp on this book! Make a copy first.) Give it a try. You may like how it feels to show them who's boss.

In addition to knowing what the Worry Weasels look like, you also need to recognize their voices. The Worry Weasels love to whisper scary or unhelpful thoughts in your head. They may say things like, *You're not going to make the team,* or *Bad things are going to happen to you.* You will have to listen very carefully to hear them. You may need to take a day to just listen and hear what they are saying.

The Bible says in James 1:17, "Every good and perfect gift is from above, coming down from the Father of the heavenly lights, who does not change like shifting shadows." Good things are from God. Anything negative or hurtful is not from God. God wants you to know that you are special, loved, and His. Any thoughts that tell you something different are not from your Father in Heaven, Who loves you.

On the following page, in the box on the left, write down the kinds of things you hear the Worry Weasels saying to you in your head. In the box on the right, rewrite the negative message so that it is a positive message. An example is provided for you.

WORRY WEASEL MESSAGES	POSITIVE MESSAGES
1. You missed that goal and cost your team the game. You are so bad.	1. I am not bad. Sure, I wish we had won, but I played my best.

You may be wondering if you are strong enough to fight off the Worry Weasels. You are! Remember, "'with God, all things are possible'" (Matt. 19:26)! As you work through the rest of this workbook, you will be collecting weapons along the way that will help you fight back. These weapons will help you break into the worry cycle and kick those Worry Weasels out. You are going to feel much better very soon. So, put on your battle gear.

IT'S TIME TO WAGE WAR!

SECTION 3

TIME FOR WAR!

Wow! You have learned a lot so far! You now know:
- What happens in your brain when you worry
- How you feel worry in your body
- The kinds of things you tend to worry about
- How worry affects you and your family
- What your Worry Weasels look and sound like

Now that you know all this information, it is time to put it to use! The next several pages contain information and activities that will give you all the weapons you need to win the war on worry. It helps if you do them in order, one at a time, over a period of three weeks or so, but do what feels right to you. You can check them off on this page as you go along.

☐ Battle #1: Ready, Set, Breathe!

☐ Battle #2: Don't Just Stand There—Get Moving!

☐ Battle #3: Create Peace—Use Your Imagination!

- [ ] Battle #4: Rounding Up the Enemy—Create a Worry Box
- [ ] Battle #5: Avoid Surprise Attacks—Schedule Your Worry Time
- [ ] Battle #6: Train for Battle—Food, Water, Sleep, and Exercise
- [ ] Battle #7: Start Off Your Day Right—Put On the Armor of God
- [ ] Battle #8: Don't Get Brainwashed—Take Every Thought Captive!
- [ ] Battle #9: Face the Truth With Thanks
- [ ] Battle #10: Stand Your Ground—Look Your Worries in the Eye

BATTLE #1: READY, SET, BREATHE!

Remember that worry cycle? (Flip back and review it if you don't.) In these first three battles, you are going to learn about some very important weapons that will break into the worry cycle and kick those Worry Weasels out. Today's weapon is BREATHING.

Breathing is something that is involuntary or instinctive. You don't have to tell yourself to breathe. Your body just knows how to do it because that is how God designed you. You need oxygen to live, and breathing gets it into your body. With the fight-or-flight response, your breathing can get all messed up. You may start breathing really fast, hold your breath, or take shallow breaths. Any of these can make you feel lightheaded, dizzy, and more nervous.

Even though breathing is automatic, you can gain control over it when you want. Try this:

Hold your breath.

Now let it out.

Breathe in slowly two times.

Now push all the air out of your lungs.

See? You can control your own breathing! There are two things you are going to be able to do after this activity today—control how fast you breathe and control where you breathe.

SLOW IT DOWN

As we talked about before, worried people's breathing is often fast and shallow. Maybe fast breathing was one of the worry body signals you picked earlier. Since you now know that you can control your breathing, you will just have to spend some time practicing. First, you will need to slow down your breathing and inhale deeply. Even if you didn't select fast breathing as one of your worry body signals, learning how to control your breathing is good practice for anyone who battles the Worry Weasels.

For starters, take a nice, deep breath and slowly let it out. Stretch your arms up toward the ceiling as you breathe in and relax them as you breathe out. If you feel dizzy or lightheaded, you may have breathed in too fast or let it out too fast. You should not feel dizzy, just relaxed. Try it again slowly until you feel calm and relaxed. Have your parent practice with you.

IDENTIFY THE SOURCE

Now, lie on the floor or a sofa and place one hand on your chest and one on your stomach. Breathe normally. Which part of your body do you feel going up and down as you breathe? Even though your lungs are in your chest, the best kind of breathing happens when your stomach goes up and down (or in and out if you are standing). Try to breathe deeply and slowly until your stomach, not your chest, goes up and down with each breath.

Don't worry if you can't figure it out right away. It may take some practice.

MAKE EVERY BREATH COUNT!

Once you have mastered this kind of stomach breathing, you can put it into practice any time you need to. One easy way is with a breath prayer. By just saying two simple phrases—one when you breathe in and one when you breathe out—you can kick out any anxious thoughts or feelings.

Here's an example of a breath prayer:

As you take a slow, deep, stomach breath through your nose, say to yourself, "God is with me." As you let it out through your lips, say to yourself, "He will never, ever leave my side."

You can come up with any prayer or positive message you want. One tip is to make sure that the second phrase has more syllables than the first. This will cause you to let the air out more slowly than you took it in, which will help you relax even more.

Work with your parent to come up with a breath prayer that is helpful to you. Once you have figured it out, write it here:

PLAN AHEAD

A soldier needs to be prepared. Going into battle without proper preparation can mean disaster. The same is true in the war against worry. Think about some different situations when you might be able to use your breath prayer to battle your anxious thoughts. Planning ahead like this will make it easier to break the cycle of worry before you have gone around too many times. Below, write down one situation in which you think a breath prayer would be helpful to you.

I think a breath prayer would be helpful when: _____

_____

_____

_____

_____.

Another great time to use this tool is when you are experiencing some of those worry body signals you picked out earlier. Dizzy or lightheaded? Say a breath prayer. Feeling shaky or have butterflies in your stomach? Say a breath prayer. The breathing rhythm will slow down your mind and body and give you something to concentrate on besides those pesky Worry Weasels and your worry body signals.

BATTLE #2: DON'T JUST STAND THERE—GET MOVING!

Sometimes, when your body wants to fight back or run away, one of the best things you can do is to give your body something to do with all that pent-up energy. EXERCISE to the rescue! Exercising can quickly break into that worry cycle and calm you down by helping your body use up all that "worry energy." And if you imagine that with every step you are squashing a Worry Weasel, it will be even more fun!

Think about the things you like to do to get out your energy. Some ideas are listed below. Circle the ones that are enjoyable to you. Add a few ideas of your own!

RUNNING	DANCING	GYMNASTICS
RIDING A BICYCLE	SWINGING	MARTIAL ARTS
JUMPING ROPE	ROLLER SKATING	JUMPING ON TRAMPOLINE
RIDING A SCOOTER	RAKING LEAVES	BASEBALL
JUMPING JACKS	SKATEBOARDING	SOCCER

BASKETBALL	FOOTBALL	PULL-UPS
HOPSCOTCH	HIKING IN THE WOODS	GAMES OF TAG
SWIMMING	FRISBEE	

All of these activities are great ways to get rid of your worry energy and fight off the Worry Weasels. Any time you feel caught in the worry cycle, give one of these activities a try. We will talk more about the importance of regular exercise in a later battle.

But what if you can't do one of these activities? What if you are in the middle of class at school?

Some kids will use more subtle movements in order to get rid of extra energy that comes from being worried. Unfortunately, many of these are harmful to you or disruptive to others. These include:

- Biting fingernails
- Jiggling legs or feet
- Grinding or clenching teeth
- Chewing on pens or pencils
- Chewing on collars or hair
- Tapping pens or pencils on a table

Have you done any of these before? Maybe you are even doing one right now. If you find yourself doing one of these unhelpful activities, replace it with a helpful one listed below. Try out each one as you read through them. Be sure to remember your breathing as you do them!

- Squeeze your fists, hold for ten seconds, then release.
- Curl your toes in your shoes five times.
- Twist your head slowly from side to side three times.
- Lift your foot up and down, very slowly, ten times.
- Give yourself a bear hug.
- Slowly nod your head to the beat of a song in your head.
- Chew gum (if you are allowed).

Now that you have learned some helpful alternatives, you can use any of these more subtle stress-relievers any time you need to. If you are in class or on the bus, you can easily curl your toes or squeeze your fists to get rid of some of that nervous energy.

Below, list some places that you could use these more subtle techniques: _____

_____

_____

_____

In the next day or two, try them out. Write the one that works best for you here: _____

_____

_____

BATTLE #3: CREATE PEACE— USE YOUR IMAGINATION!

So, you already have two weapons to help you break the worry cycle—breathing and exercising. During this session, you will learn about the last tool—iMAgiNATioN.

The following passage is from Revelation. The author (Jesus' disciple John) had a vision from God. In his vision, he was taken to Heaven. Afterward, he tried to write down all that he saw. It wasn't easy because Heaven is nothing like earth. As you read through the passage, underline all the words he used to describe Heaven. Then have your parent read it to you again as you close your eyes and imagine the scene that John described.

> Then the angel showed me the river of the water of life, as clear as crystal, flowing from the throne of God and of the Lamb down the middle of the great street of the city. On each side of the river stood the tree of life, bearing twelve crops of fruit, yielding its fruit every month. And the leaves of the tree are for the healing of the nations. No longer will there be any curse. The throne of God and of the Lamb

will be in the city, and his servants will serve him. They will see his face, and his name will be on their foreheads. There will be no more night. They will not need the light of a lamp or the light of the sun, for the Lord God will give them light. And they will reign for ever and ever (Rev. 22:1-5).

Now, get some crayons, colored pencils, or markers. Turn this workbook sideways, and on the next page, draw the scene you imagined. The more detail, the better.

Look over the picture and think about where you would want to be if you were part of that scene. Draw yourself in that spot. Take a mental snapshot of the completed picture and find somewhere comfortable where you can lie down. Lie down, close your eyes, and imagine that you are right there, inside your picture. Imagine that Jesus is there, too, sitting or walking with you. Have your parent ask you the following questions and record your answers as you imagine yourself inside the scene you drew.

What do you hear?_____
_____
_____
_____.

What do you smell? _____
_____
_____
_____.

What feelings do you have?_____
_____
_____
_____.

Who else is with you?_____
_____
_____
_____.

This scene can now be your "peaceful spot." Anytime your thoughts feel trapped in the cycle of worry, you can break out. All you have to do is close your eyes and imagine this peaceful spot with Jesus. You can do this no matter where or with whom you are. As you do so, ask God to give you peace.

If you are struggling to use this tool on your own when you are worried, ask your parent to help you. Close your eyes and allow your parent to describe, in detail, what they see in the picture you drew. Listen as they speak and try to imagine that you are walking through the scene they describe.

God wants you to experience this kind of peace. He holds that peace out to you as a free gift. Grab it!

Memorize this verse, so you will have it wherever you go:

"AND THE PEACE OF GOD, WHICH TRANSCENDS ALL UNDERSTANDING, WILL GUARD YOUR HEARTS AND YOUR MINDS IN CHRIST JESUS" (PHIL. 4:7).

BATTLE #4: ROUNDING UP THE ENEMY—CREATE A WORRY BOX

Anxious thoughts can feel unpredictable. They can pop up any time, unannounced and uninvited. In order to win the war on worry, you will need to collect them all in one place so you can keep an eye on them. That is where the worry box comes in. In this battle, you will create a worry box to help you contain the different worries as they pop into your head.

WHAT YOU WILL NEED:
- Shoe box or small cardboard box
- Wrapping paper or plain paper bag
- Paints, markers, crayons
- Scissors or box knife (FOR PARENTS ONLY)
- Index cards
- Bible
- Pen

INSTRUCTIONS:

1. Wrap the box in wrapping paper or a plain paper bag. Make sure that you wrap the top and bottom separately.
2. Have a parent CAREFULLY cut a slit in the top of the box a little wider than the width of an index card.
3. Decorate the box.
4. Add some (or all) of the Scripture verses below to the outside of the box. Use your Bible to see if you can find any more of your own. Ask your parent to help.

- "Therefore do not worry about tomorrow, for tomorrow will worry about itself. Each day has enough trouble of its own" (Matt. 6:34).
- "Peace I leave with you; my peace I give you. I do not give to you as the world gives. Do not let your hearts be troubled and do not be afraid" (John 14:27).
- "Cast your cares on the LORD and he will sustain you; he will never let the righteous be shaken" (Psalm 55:22).
- "Cast all your anxiety on him because he cares for you" (1 Peter 5:7).
- "When I am afraid, I put my trust in you" (Psalm 56:3).

HOW TO USE YOUR WORRY BOX

As you go through your day and worries pop into your head, write them down on the index cards. (If you want, draw your image of a Worry Weasel on the cards, too.) You may need the help of your parent at first if you don't remember to use the worry box all the time. Don't get upset with them. They are supposed to remind you.

Every time you put a card in the box, read one of the Bible verses on the side of the box. Keep the box somewhere handy. You will need it for the next battle.

BATTLE #5: AVOID SURPRISE ATTACKS—SCHEDULE YOUR WORRY TIME

The Worry Weasels are such pests! They love to keep those worries stuck in the worry cycle going round and round getting bigger all the time. In battles one through three, you learned how to kick them out with breathing, exercising, and using your imagination. But today's weapon will help you beat them at their own game by stopping the worries from even entering the worry cycle. From now on, you are going to schedule your worry time.

"What? That doesn't make any sense!" you may say. "I thought the whole point of this was to worry less, not make time in my day to worry!"

It may sound strange, but let's think about it for a minute. Right now, how many minutes (or hours) a day do you think you spend worrying? Probably a lot. For some people, worries are always playing in the background of their minds, kind of like the music at a dentist's office. By scheduling time to worry each day, you will actually be worrying less overall.

Pushing aside worries may seem like a bad idea. Most grown-ups know that ignoring something is not a good way to make it better. But in this case, you are definitely *not* ignoring your worries. You are simply setting them aside until a later time. You are in charge. Follow the steps below.

1. PICK A TIME.

At first, give yourself two worry "appointments" each day of about fifteen minutes each. At the beginning of the day, decide when those appointments will be (not before bedtime), and make sure a parent is available during those times in case you need them. These are important appointments, so don't miss them!

Write the two times you picked here:
Appointment #1: _____
Appointment #2: _____

2. COLLECT YOUR WORRIES.

As you go through your day, write or draw your worries on index cards. When you put them in your worry box, read the Scriptures and tell yourself, "I don't need to worry about this now. I will have time to worry about it later."

3. KEEP YOUR APPOINTMENT.

At your scheduled appointment time, with a parent nearby, take your worry box and a Bible to a quiet place (like your room or outside under a tree). Open the lid and take out the worries one at a time.

4. TALK IT OUT.

Next, name each of your worries out loud. This part is very important. Have you ever been in your bedroom at night and thought you saw something scary across the room? But then you flicked on the light and saw it was just your jacket hanging on the back of your chair. Ephesians 5:13 says, "But everything exposed by the light becomes visible—and everything that is illuminated becomes a light." Saying your worries out loud is a bit like turning on the lights. It will make your worries seem smaller. It will expose them to the truth, and it will take away their power.

Remember that decision-making part of your brain? These following questions are going to help you exercise that part and make it stronger. Discuss the answers with your parent.

- What *exactly* am I worried about?
- When did this worry start?
- How likely is it that this worry will happen?
- Is there anything I can actually *do* about this worry?

You might want to write these four questions on an index card and tape it to the bottom of your worry box. That way, every time you have your worry appointment, the questions will be right there.

5. LOOK TO GOD'S WORD.

Finally, ask your parent to help you find Bible verses about each type of worry. Use an online concordance (a

Bible dictionary) and write any verses you find on the back of the card.

If you are really struggling to put your worry out of your mind until your appointment, talk to your parent and have them help you use one of the first three weapons you collected—breathing, exercising, and using your imagination. You've got this!

Over time, you will find that you need to schedule fewer and fewer appointments with your worries. In fact, you may find that you can't even use all of the fifteen minutes because you have run out of things to worry about!

Now it's time to write about your very first worry appointment. Answer these questions when it is over:

1. Waiting for the appointment was:

VERY HARD   NOT TOO BAD   EASIER THAN I THOUGHT   SUPER EASY

2. This is where I decided to have my worry appointment: _____

3. Saying my worries out loud was:

VERY AWKWARD   A LITTLE WEIRD   NOT THAT BAD   VERY HELPFUL

4. After my appointment, I felt _____

5. This is what I realized about my worry during my appointment: _____

_____

_____

_____

BATTLE #6: TRAIN FOR BATTLE— FOOD, WATER, SLEEP, AND EXERCISE

We've talked before about the fact that any good soldier needs to be prepared for battle. Have you ever seen soldiers train? They work really hard! They exercise a lot, eat healthy food, perform lots of drills, and train their minds to focus on the task at hand.

When you are fighting the Worry Weasels, you also need to be in tip-top shape. For the next two days, keep a log of how you are taking care of your body. Write down what you eat, how much water you drink, how many hours you sleep, and how much and what kind of exercise you get. Two additional charts are included in the back of the book that you can tear out and keep somewhere you will remember to complete it. It's okay if your parent helps you remember to fill it out. They are just doing their job.

DAY 1

FOOD

Breakfast: _____

Lunch: _____

Dinner: _____

Snacks _____

WATER (Make a check each time you drink eight ounces of water.)

☐ ☐ ☐ ☐ ☐ ☐ ☐ ☐

SLEEP

Number of hours: _____

EXERCISE

What activities I did: _____

How long I did them: _____

DAY 2

FOOD

Breakfast: _____

Lunch: _____

Dinner: _____

Snacks _____

WATER (Make a check each time you drink eight ounces of water.)

☐ ☐ ☐ ☐ ☐ ☐ ☐ ☐

SLEEP

Number of hours: _____

EXERCISE

What activities I did: _____

How long I did them: _____

Now that you have completed the chart, it's time to do a little comparing. Listed below are three different kinds of soldiers. Some are more ready for battle than others. They are:

- The Ready Recruit
- The Partially Prepared Private
- The Sluggish Serviceperson

THE READY RECRUIT is ready for whatever the day hands him. He gets his day off right with a hearty breakfast. He makes sure he gets some protein (meats, cheese, eggs, fish or nuts) at every meal to fuel his day. Vegetables and fruits are common on his plate. He loves to drink milk and water to quench his thirst. He enjoys a sweet treat once in a while but knows when he has had enough. (He doesn't like how sugar makes him feel energetic for a few minutes but then tired for much longer.) He exercises for about thirty to sixty minutes a day. (He particularly likes running the obstacle course!) He makes sure to get plenty of sleep at night—up to nine hours!

THE PARTIALLY PREPARED PRIVATE has good days and bad days. Sometimes, he doesn't get to bed on time. He usually wakes up to an alarm, never feeling quite rested enough. He loves video games and sometimes convinces himself that playing them counts as exercise. He eats cereal or toast for breakfast, plain pasta for lunch, and chicken nuggets with a side of baby carrots for dinner. He'd rather drink juice than water, but he will drink water, as long as it's flavored.

THE SLUGGISH SERVICEPERSON is always tired. He stays up really late reading comics, and his commander has to drag him out of bed each day. He eats donuts for breakfast, a hot dog for lunch, and usually pizza and soda for dinner. You will often find him with a pack of Smarties® in his hand—although he hasn't been doing that great on his tests lately, so he is starting to wonder if they are really working.

Now, take a moment and compare your daily logs to these three different soldiers. Which of the three are you most like? Are you ready, partially prepared, or too sluggish to care?

If you are most like the Ready Recruit, congratulations! You are on the right track. Keep up the good work, taking care of the body that God has given you.

If you are more like the Partially Prepared Private, you have some room for improvement. Don't try to make all the changes at once. Pick one area and work on that first. Circle which area you will work on first:

EAT BETTER   DRINK MORE WATER   GET MORE SLEEP   EXERCISE MORE

Now, if you are more like the Sluggish Serviceperson, you might need to start from scratch. Maybe you can encourage your family to start the journey toward healthier living with you. Sit down together and talk about ways that you can improve in the areas of healthy eating, sleeping, and exercise. If you are going to win the war against worry, you need to be in the very best shape possible. Having a whole family filled with Ready Recruits will make the battles much easier to win. Check out healthychildren.org for more great tips on staying healthy.

Next, grab your Bible and look up 1 Corinthians 6:19-20. Write it here:

_____
_____
_____
_____
_____
_____
_____
_____

What does "our bodies are a temple" mean? It sounds weird, but it's pretty simple. The Jewish people saw the temple (their name for their church) as the place where God lived. When Paul (the writer of Corinthians) said that our bodies are a temple, he was simply saying that our bodies are where God lives. Do you want to know God's address? Pull out the collar of your shirt and look down. He lives in YOU! And that makes your body worth caring for!

BATTLE #7: START OFF YOUR DAY RIGHT—PUT ON THE ARMOR OF GOD

All the physical preparation in the world isn't going to help you if you aren't prepared spiritually. How do you prepare spiritually to fight off the Worry Weasels? You start your day with some time with God. Having that time with God in the morning has a way of setting your day off right.

"GOOD MORNING, GOD!"

Your mornings may be busy, so here's a really easy way you can start your day with God. Before you go to bed at night, make sure your Bible is somewhere you can reach it from your bed. Have a flashlight or headlamp available in case it is dark when you get up in the morning. When your alarm (or parent) wakes you up, open your Bible and read ten verses. Or if you are feeling really ambitious, read a whole chapter. If your parent is willing, he or she could read it with you. It's important to have a version of the Bible that you can understand. You may really like the Contemporary English Version (CEV) or the New International Version (NIV).

If you don't know where to start reading, start in Psalms. David (the author of many of the psalms) battled Worry

Weasels, too. Once you have read a passage and understand it, shut your Bible, close your eyes, and pray about what you read.

- Thank God if He gave you comfort.
- Praise God if He reminded you of how mighty He is.
- Ask God to help you trust Him like the psalmist did.

Then, turn your day over to God by saying, "It's in Your hands, God!" as you hop out of bed.

GET DRESSED GOD'S WAY!

As you get dressed, you can also put on a suit of armor. There are some verses in the Bible that are just perfect for a soldier headed off to battle. Ephesians six talks about "putting on the armor of God." What a great passage to study if you are going to do battle with the Worry Weasels! Read the passage below, and underline the different parts of armor.

> Finally, be strong in the Lord and in his mighty power . . . Therefore put on the full armor of God, so that when the day of evil comes, you may be able to stand your ground, and after you have done everything, to stand. Stand firm then, with the belt of truth buckled around your waist, with the breastplate of righteousness in place, and with your feet fitted with the readiness that comes from the

gospel of peace. In addition to all this, take up the shield of faith, with which you can extinguish all the flaming arrows of the evil one. Take the helmet of salvation and the sword of the Spirit, which is the word of God" (Eph. 6:10, 13-17).

Did you find them all? There are five—belt, breastplate, shield, helmet, and sword. When you get dressed in the morning, you can put on God's armor right along with your clothes! Here's how:

1. BELT OF TRUTH

First, put on your pants and tighten your belt. Think of all the things that you know to be true about who you are in Christ. Here are a few to get you started:
- I am a friend of God (Eph. 2:13; John 15:15).
- God chose me; I am important to Him (1 Peter 2:9).
- My sins have been paid for (Col. 2:14-15).
- God has a plan for me (Jer. 29:11).

2. BREASTPLATE OF RIGHTEOUSNESS

As you tug your shirt over your head, thank God that you are protected because you are in "right" relationship with Him. That's what righteousness means. Just like a shirt covers you, Jesus' death on the cross covered all of your sins so you could have a "right" relationship with God (2 Cor. 5:21).

3. SHIELD OF FAITH

If you need a sweater or a jacket, put it on and imagine it as a warm covering of faith that protects you like a shield. What is faith, you ask? Hebrews 11:1 tells us, "Now faith is confidence in what we hope for and assurance about what we do not see." You can have hope that you will have a future not overcome with worry. And you can have assurance that even though you can't see God, His love surrounds you every step of the way.

4. HELMET OF SALVATION

Just for fun, put on a hat. As you do so, remind yourself that you are saved from your sins. If you haven't made a decision to follow Jesus yet, now would be a great time to talk to your parent about it. You can have assurance of where you are heading when your time on earth is done because you believe in the Son of God (1 John 5:13).

5. SWORD OF THE SPIRIT

Now that you are dressed, grab your Bible, look at yourself in the mirror, and raise the Bible with triumph in the air. This is your sword, and it really is the best weapon of all.

Do you remember the story of Jesus when He was tempted in the desert? How did He fight off Satan? With Scripture! (You can read all about it in Matthew chapter four.) When Worry Weasels try to make your worries grow, you, too, can fight them off with the sword of Scripture.

Below are some worries. Match them up with a Bible verse that could be used to fight back. There may be more than one right answer.

MY WORRY	SCRIPTURE TO FIGHT BACK
I AM AFRAID OF GETTING SICK.	"AND SURELY I AM WITH YOU ALWAYS, TO THE VERY END OF THE AGE" (MATT. 28:20)
I AM WORRIED THAT I WON'T MAKE ANY FRIENDS.	"WHOEVER BELIEVES IN [JESUS] SHALL NOT PERISH BUT HAVE ETERNAL LIFE" (JOHN 3:16).
I AM NERVOUS ABOUT FAILING MY TEST TOMORROW.	"YOU ARE MY FRIENDS IF YOU DO WHAT I COMMAND" (JOHN 15:14).
I AM WORRIED THAT I AM GOING TO GET LOST.	"I CAN DO ALL THIS THROUGH [GOD] WHO GIVES ME STRENGTH" (PHIL. 4:13).

What verses help you in your battle against worry? List them below.

On the following page is a drawing of a soldier dressed in God's armor, ready for battle. On it, write what each piece of armor represents. Tear out the drawing and put it where you can see it as you get ready each morning. Use it to help you remember God's way of getting dressed.

BATTLE #8: DON'T GET BRAINWASHED—TAKE EVERY THOUGHT CAPTIVE!

There is an interesting verse in 2 Corinthians that says, "We take captive every thought to make it obedient to Christ" (2 Cor. 10:5). Because we are thinking in terms of waging a war against worry, this verse is very helpful. You've already learned that you can't run from or fight your worries because they are just thoughts and feelings. But maybe you can capture them. Would you like to try?

One of the best ways to take a worry captive is to trap it with REASON. Remember that decision-making part of your brain? Get it ready. You're going to need it! The following exercise will help you capture any anxious thought you may face.

The first thing you need to do is think of a time when you were worried. Maybe you were afraid to leave the house. Maybe you were worried that your dad wouldn't come home from work. For this exercise, it has to be a specific worry—not just a general "I felt nervous" situation.

In the space below, describe a specific worry you had in the past and then write down what actually happened.

One day in the past, I was worried that this would happen:

_____
_____
_____
_____
_____
_____
_____

But as it turned out, this is what actually happened:

_____
_____
_____
_____
_____
_____
_____

Now, talk with your parent about a specific worry you are facing right now. Write it here:

I am worried that _____
_____.

Using the following chart, try to figure out what is the best, worst, and most likely outcome from this specific worry. You can ask your parent to walk you through this, but the answers should be your own. The ideas have to come from you if you are going to take the worry captive.

This would be the *best* possible outcome from this worry:	This would be the *worst* possible outcome from this worry:	This is the *most likely* outcome from this worry:

The thing about Worry Weasels is that they trick you into *only* thinking about the middle column, the worst possible outcome. They make you think there is no other option, and pretty soon, that fight-or-flight response had kicked in. You can show them who's boss by realizing that there are other outcomes.

When you feel attacked by a Worry Weasel, stop and respond to him by using some or all of these thoughts from the decision-making part of your brain:

- *Come on. How likely is that going to happen? I have been in this situation before, and it didn't turn out like that.*
- *The chance of that actually happening is so small!*
- *Usually, things turn out better than I can imagine.*

- *You will not trick me into thinking only about the worst-case scenario.*
- *God is always with me, so I don't have to be afraid of that outcome.*

If you use one of these, you will likely find the Worry Weasel tongue-tied with no response. Whenever you sense that you are focusing on the worst possible outcome, remember that you can *choose* to think about it differently.

Another thing that Worry Weasels like to do is exaggerate. They like to use words like "always" and "never." Here are some examples:

- *You are never going to make any friends.*
- *You are always wrong.*

Pay attention to these types of words, the ones that leave no room for any exceptions. If you start to hear them in your head, you can be sure that a Worry Weasel is behind that thought. Take it captive with a counter-attack. You can say something like:

- *Never is a long time. That is pretty unlikely.*
- *I can't always be wrong. Just yesterday, I got nine out of ten answers correct on my spelling test!*

Remember, your brain is yours. Don't let the Worry Weasels hijack it with false information and exaggeration. You have the truth of the Lord on your side. Truth always *defeats* lies. And that's no exaggeration!

BATTLE #9: FACE THE TRUTH WITH THANKS

There was a little boy who used to worry that there was a giraffe outside his bedroom window at night. Keep in mind that where he lived, there were no giraffes around. Ever. But he was worried just the same. A lot of worries are like that. We *know* that they just can't happen, but they certainly *feel* like they could.

But what do you do if you have a worry about something that might actually happen? Maybe you have concerns about your mom's job. Or maybe you are worried about someone in your family. Let's call these "what if" worries.

The truth is that no matter if the "what if" worry is possible or not, you can still use all the skills you have learned throughout this workbook. In fact, you might be able to teach the adults in your life who face similar worries how to use some of the weapons you have collected!

But sometimes, these types of worries require a bit more attention. As always, the best place to find solutions to life's problems is in the Bible. Let's look a little closer at a verse about worry that is probably pretty familiar to you:

"DO NOT BE ANXIOUS ABOUT ANYTHING, BUT IN EVERY SITUATION, BY PRAYER AND PETITION, WITH THANKSGIVING, PRESENT YOUR REQUESTS TO GOD" (PHIL. 4:6).

What does Paul say we should do when we are anxious? Pray! We pray to God because we know He is the greatest Helper of all. There is another very helpful little tip tucked in this verse that you may have passed right over when you read it. It comes after the word "with," and it has nothing to do with turkey and stuffing. That word is . . . THANKSGIVING.

It is very difficult to stay stuck in a state of worry if you fill your head with all the things for which you are thankful. Here's a fun craft that you can make that will help you keep your mind focused on thanks instead of on "what if" worries.

SUPPLIES YOU NEED:

- Small branch from a tree or sticks
- Vase with a block of florist foam or small rocks to hold the branch upright
- Colored construction paper
- Hole punch
- String
- Pencil or pen
- Envelope

HOW TO MAKE A THANKFUL TREE:

- Using your pencil or pen, draw different leaf shapes onto the construction paper. (Alternatively,

you could print out images from the internet.) Cut the leaves out.
- On one side of each leaf, write something for which you are thankful. You can use this format if you'd like: "I am thankful for _____ because _____."
- Punch a hole in the top of each leaf, thread a piece of string through it, and tie it off, making a loop.
- On the envelope, write this verse from 1 Chronicles 16:34: "Give thanks to the LORD, for he is good; his love endures forever."
- Store your leaves in the envelope.
- Push the branch or sticks into the center of the rocks or florist foam, making sure you have places to hang your leaves.

How To Use It:
- Every time you experience a "what if" worry, grab a leaf out of the envelope.
- Hold the leaf and say this prayer (or use your own words):

    > *Lord, I am worried about _____. I know that You care. I know that You hear me. I pray that You would _____. Help me to trust You.*

- Read out loud what you have written on the leaf, and hang it on your tree. Keep repeating this process until you have a sense of peace and protection from the One Who has given you everything and loves you so much.

If you have trouble coming up with things to write on your leaves, talk to your parent. Sometimes, it helps to have a reminder or two. You could also go back through this workbook and practice some of the calming techniques you have learned. You may have to say a breath prayer or imagine your peaceful spot to quiet those Worry Weasels so the thankful thoughts can be heard.

BATTLE #10: STAND YOUR GROUND— LOOK YOUR WORRIES IN THE EYE

Soldiers are pretty amazing people. When they face dangerous circumstances, surely their instincts are screaming at them to run as fast as they can. But they don't. They stay and fight. This next battle is probably going to be a bit uncomfortable, but you have so many weapons in your pocket now. You, too, are a trained soldier, and you are ready to face the enemy head on!

Here is a true story about a young boy who became very anxious when he saw a blank piece of paper. Obviously, this isn't a common worry, but it just goes to show you that they come in all shapes and sizes. As you can imagine, being afraid of blank paper can be a big problem if you are a student in school. Clearly, something had to be done. He spent some time learning and using all the same weapons as you. Then, with the help of his mom and a friend, he made a plan to practice facing his worries.

He started small. On the first day, he sat in a chair, with his mom nearby. A blank piece of paper was placed on the table in front of him. He agreed to keep it there for just one minute to start. That was a long minute! But he was armed and ready. He calmed his body with deep, slow breathing and muscle squeezes and fought off those Worry Weasels. Each time he practiced facing his worries, he could go longer and longer with the paper in front of him until, eventually, it didn't bother him at all.

Maybe you have a worry that is holding you back, something you are avoiding or that makes you anxious to even think about. It's time to gear up and go to war! Here are the steps you can follow:

1. AGREE

First you need to make an agreement with your parent. When you are ready, sign the statement below:

> I, _____ (your name), do hereby agree to use all my weapons to practice fighting my worry face to face. I know it might be uncomfortable, but I also know that can I do it.

Your Signature _____

Parent Signature _____

2. COLLECT YOUR WEAPONS.

Make a list of all the weapons you plan to use during this battle. List them here: _____
_____
_____

3. MAKE A BATTLE PLAN.

Now is the time for some decisions. First, decide exactly what fear you want to face and then think of all the little steps you could take to get there, from easiest to hardest. Talk about it with your parent and write the steps of your plan on a separate piece of paper. If you are stuck, the following example might help

Let's say you are extremely afraid of bees. You could start facing your worry by looking at a picture of a bee for thirty seconds one day. The next day, you could try increasing the amount of time you look at the picture. Once the picture doesn't bother you, you could move on to videos of bees. You might start with just thirty seconds and work your way up. Next, you could find a beekeeper and ask to see a bee behind glass. You would continue this process until you could be outside, and bees no longer prevented you from having fun.

Be sure to use your weapons to calm your body during every step of your plan.

4. BE PATIENT!

This process can take some time, so don't get discouraged if it takes a while or if you get stuck at one stage for a bit. You can take a break for a day if you need to, but don't give up. You can do it! (Note to parents: pay attention to your own feelings during this process so you can portray confidence. Furthermore, if you find your child is really struggling with this activity, don't push him. Give him time to adjust to the process and then revisit it at a later date.)

THE FINAL VERDICT: REMEMBER—THE WAR'S ALREADY WON

Have you ever watched an adventure movie and found yourself on the edge of your seat because you didn't know how it was going to turn out? And have you ever watched that same movie a second time and noticed how you were excited but didn't have that same sense of concern? That's because the second time through, you knew exactly how the movie was going to end.

The same is true when God looks at your life. He knows how the story of your life turns out because He wrote it. He doesn't get nervous or bite His nails when He sees you struggle because He knows that, in the end, you are a winner.

Below are some truths taken right from the Bible. They can help you remember that no matter what battles you face today, no matter what those Worry Weasels say or do, God has proclaimed you a winner. Stand up and read the following statements out loud with confidence!

- God helps me win my battles (Deut. 20:4)!
- I can do anything with God by my side (Phil. 4:13)!

- Jesus Christ gives me the victory (1 Cor. 15:57)!
- Because I am a child of God, I have overcome the world (1 John 5:4-5)!

Never forget that, in God's eyes, you are "MORE THAN A CONQUEROR," and the war is already won!

SECTION 4

THE ENEMY SURRENDERS! YOU'VE WON!

Congratulations! You have collected all of the weapons you need and have fought so hard along the way. It is time to celebrate!

VICTORY IS YOURS!

You didn't just win the war against worry; you filled your toolbelt to overflowing with helpful weapons to use against those Worry Weasels anytime you need.

Let's take a moment to review. Here are all the weapons you now have at your fingertips to battle the Worry Weasels:

- You can use breathing exercises, like a breath prayer.
- You can turn nervous energy into physical exercise.
- You can imagine your peaceful spot.
- You can write your worries down and put them in your box.

- You can tell your worries they have to wait for an appointment.
- You can make sure to take care of your body.
- You can put on God's armor every morning.
- You can fight off your worries with reason.
- You can pray with a thankful heart.
- You can defeat your worries by looking them in the eye.

What are some things that you felt were most helpful to you in this workbook?

_____
_____
_____
_____
_____
_____
_____

On a scale from one to ten, how much were the Worry Weasels bothering you before you started this workbook? Circle the number ("1" being "very little" and "10" being "all the time").

1   2   3   4   5   6   7   8   9   10

Now, circle the number that shows how much it feels like they are bothering you today.

1   2   3   4   5   6   7   8   9   10

That number is probably a lot lower now. (Note to parents: if the number is not lower, now would be a good time to get some help from a trusted counselor.)

Take a moment to thank God for the work He has done in your life. You are so precious to Him, and He rejoices with you in your victory over worry.

Now that you have completed this book, you need to celebrate. Think of some different things that you could do to celebrate the work that God has done in your life to help you fight off the Worry Weasels. List some ideas here:

_____
_____
_____
_____
_____
_____

Talk to your parent and make a plan to do one of these activities within the next week. You have worked hard, and all soldiers need a little rest and relaxation! At the end of this book, you will find a certificate. Fill it out and hang it somewhere in your room as a proud reminder of all the hard work you have done.

KEEP YOUR GUARD(S) UP

Before we go, there is one last thing we need to discuss. Have you ever heard the phrase "keep your guard up"? Well, when fighting the war against worry, you will need to keep your *guards* up. Just like sentries guard a castle, you need to make sure that you have some security in place to protect you in the future.

Here are some tips to keep those Worry Weasels out of your castle and hold onto the progress you have made so far:

1. ALWAYS HAVE REINFORCEMENTS NEARBY.

Make sure that you always have someone in your life whom you trust and will be there for you, day or night, if you need help. This person should know about all the different weapons you have learned to use and all the battles you've won.

2. DON'T BE AFRAID TO ASK FOR HELP.

Soldiers don't fight battles alone. There is nothing wrong if you find that you have slipped back a bit. Don't get upset. It is normal. But don't wait to ask for help either. God put you in your family, church, and community for a reason. Use the help they can offer you.

3. KEEP TALKING TO GOD.

Prayer is your go-to tool in your toolbelt. Go to God whenever you are feeling the Worry Weasels sneak back in. God is the best weapon you have because He never leaves you and you need no special equipment to talk to Him or feel He is near.

4. REVIEW, REVIEW, REVIEW!

This workbook is not a "won"-and-done sort of book. You should keep it handy and look it over from time to time to remind yourself of your weapons and your successes.

5. REMEMBER PAUL.

In the Bible, the apostle Paul talks about having a "thorn in his side" (not a real thorn—something troubling in his life that stayed with him). He asked God to remove it, but God didn't—even though Paul asked Him three times. In the end, Paul was able to see that it was better that He left it there. Let's read the passage where Paul talks about it:

> Three times I pleaded with the Lord to take it away from me. But he said to me, "My grace is sufficient for you, for my power is made perfect in weakness." Therefore I will boast all the more gladly about my weaknesses, so that Christ's power may rest on me. That is why, for Christ's sake, I delight in

weaknesses, in insults, in hardships, in persecutions, in difficulties. For when I am weak, then I am strong (2 Cor. 12:8-10).

Before you started this book, your worries may have seemed like a large, painful thorn, always there and impossible to ignore. And maybe now that you are done with this book, they are completely gone. If so, rejoice! But if you happen to find that you have a tiny sliver of worries left, don't be discouraged. It is possible that, like Paul, God may not completely remove them—and that is okay. God doesn't promise us a struggle-free life, but He does promise that He "'will never leave you . . . never . . . forsake you'" (Heb. 13:5). He is always on our side in the battles of life. And with God on our side, we have nothing to fear! That is because we remember this:

> Who shall separate us from the love of Christ? Shall trouble or hardship or persecution or famine or nakedness or danger or sword? No, in all these things we are more than conquerors through him who loved us. For I am convinced that neither death nor life, neither angels nor demons, neither the present nor the future, nor any powers, neither height nor depth, nor anything else in all creation, will be able to separate us from the love of God that is in Christ Jesus our Lord (Rom. 8:35, 37-39).

CONGRATULATIONS, CONQUEROR!

This certificate is awarded to

_____

for

great bravery and courage in your war against worry!

"I can do all things through Him who strengthens me."

- Philippians 4:13

Date: _____

ADDITIONAL DAILY LOGS
DAY 1

FOOD

    Breakfast: _____

    Lunch: _____

    Dinner: _____

    Snacks _____

WATER (Make a check each time you drink eight ounces of water.)

    ☐ ☐ ☐ ☐ ☐ ☐ ☐

SLEEP

    Number of hours: _____

EXERCISE

    What activities I did: _____

    How long I did them: _____

DAY 2

FOOD

Breakfast: _____

Lunch: _____

Dinner: _____

Snacks _____

WATER (Make a check each time you drink eight ounces of water.)

☐ ☐ ☐ ☐ ☐ ☐ ☐ ☐

SLEEP

Number of hours: _____

EXERCISE

What activities I did: _____

How long I did them: _____

RECOMMENDED RESOURCES

www.cornerstonesforparents.com/empathetic-listening

www.cornerstonesforparents.com/comfort-hurting-child-job

www.positivepsychology.com/empathic-listening

ACKNOWLEDGMENTS

I would like to thank my husband for his unwavering support and steadfastness. You are my rock. I would also like to thank my two kids. I may have been your teacher over the years, but I often found myself the one being taught. Thank you for keeping me humble. I would also like to thank my parents, who have never stopped being my biggest cheerleaders. And thank you to Marybeth, who gave me the encouragement and inspiration to see this project through to the end. I'm so thankful for all of you.

ABOUT THE AUTHOR

Laura is happily married with two children, a teenage daughter and young adult son. She became a believer at a Billy Graham Crusade when she was just ten years old and has been on a journey with the Lord ever since. She studied psychology and Christian ministries at Grove City College and went on to receive her Master of Social Work from Southern Connecticut State University. She initially worked for a non-profit clinic providing counseling for children and their families. Since then, she has been a homeschool mom, a private practice therapist, and the founder of www.cornerstonesforparents.com, a place where she can combine some of her favorite things—Scripture, writing, and parenting. She started writing *More Than a Conqueror* over six years ago, but it sat on the proverbial shelf of her laptop until the 2020 pandemic dusted it off and gave it new life. It is her prayer that children everywhere who struggle with anxiety would know that they are not alone and that God can heal their "what-if," worry-filled hearts.

For more information about
Laura Kuehn
and
More Than a Conqueror
please visit:

www.cornerstonesforparents.com

Ambassador International's mission is to magnify the Lord Jesus Christ and promote His Gospel through the written word.

We believe through the publication of Christian literature, Jesus Christ and His Word will be exalted, believers will be strengthened in their walk with Him, and the lost will be directed to Jesus Christ as the only way of salvation.

For more information about
AMBASSADOR INTERNATIONAL
please visit:

www.ambassador-international.com
@AmbassadorIntl
www.facebook.com/AmbassadorIntl

Thank you for reading this book. Please consider leaving us a review on your social media, favorite retailer's website, Goodreads or Bookbub, or our website.

More from Ambassador International

I Want a Water Buffalo for Christmas tells the journey of LeGory, a young water buffalo, who brings life to a family in dire need. Several circumstances fall into place to create the life-giving wonder of providing for those less fortunate.

Everyone has to deal with a bully at some point in life, and it can be really, really hard! Come tag along on an adventure in Laurel Wood and see how a young otter named Elliot Emerson, or E.E. for short, and his gang of friends square off with a group of bullfrog bullies on the basketball court at Dogwood Park.

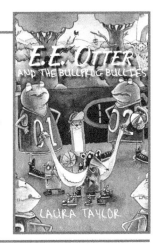

Melanie Cooper's life seems perfect. She's the star on her swim team, she has great friends, and she's turning thirteen in just a few weeks. But when her family is forced to move to Northern California, her world starts to unravel. Can Melanie learn to trust in a God that allows bad things to happen? Discover with Melanie how He can bring something good even from the difficulties in our lives.

Made in the USA
Las Vegas, NV
23 August 2023